Digital Smiles

E. Hughes

Love-LovePublishing—Madison, WI
Paperback ISBN: 978-1-961823-15-0
eBook ISBN: 978-1-961823-16-7
Title: Digital Smiles
Author: E. Hughes
Available formats: eBook
Paperback distribution

First edition

Introduction

When I wrote *Digital Smiles*, I was going through a period of disillusionment with the world and humankind. I was saddened because of the wars, especially the loss of life that included children. I was disillusioned with American society and the toxic use of social media and how it has led to a breakdown of civility and society. I was disappointed by rampant disinformation. So many people are caught in the grip and addiction of social media.

There are very few spaces where I choose to offer an opinion. I am of the belief that opinions don't change outcomes, our actions do, and it begins with changing ourselves, rather than through the expectations we place on others. But sometimes we just need to tell the gut-wrenching truth and that's why I wrote *Digital Smiles*.

Today, I limit my interactions on social media to business. It has become increasingly important to me to divest completely in social media in ways that include limiting digital interactions with strangers. This is not a movement or plea for others to do the same, but I feel that I am in a much healthier space without it. The poetry in this book was written as I observed how human beings engage each other under the cloak of anonymity where the rules of society that governs the real world is no longer applicable in these digital spaces, yet impacts us politically and socially in serious or perhaps, even catastrophic ways.

There is good and bad in all things, including social media, with moderation.

Other novels and works by E. Hughes:

Fiction:

Sixth Iteration
Disappear, Love
Business as Usual
Infatuation
A Mediterranean Romance: The Capa Royals
The Sapphire Chronicles: Broken Lair
Hello (A Screenplay)

Children's Books:

Penelope Helps Mom and Dad
Penelope: Be Kind to Animals
Penelope: Super Duper Spectacular Princess Ballerina
Penelope: Don't be afraid
Penelope Holiday Cheer
Garden of Secrets
Kissing Henry (coming soon)

Nonfiction
Time and the Multi-Universe: A philosophy of time and time travel
Starting Your First Patio Garden: A Coffee Book
Family in a Time of Covid-19: The Truth about Coronavirus, How to Protect Yourself and Prepare
Beyond the Plain (Poetry)
Reality Unbound (coming soon)

Table of Contents

Introduction..iii
Here I Stand... 1
Birds of Prey.. 2
Digital Smiles... 3
The Day is Nigh 4
Out of the Heart the Soul Speaks 5
"I'm Little and I'm Scared" 6
Disinformation 8
Meta News.. 9
An Inconvenient Sacrifice... 10
Whose Truth? 11
Spin... 12
Here 13
"US".. 14
Night I Come Hither to Thee 15
I Was Never Here... 16
When I was Young 17
Saturate.. 18
Curtain Call 19
I Marvel 20
Whisper... 21
Dead Roses 22
Just Biding My Time... 23
Why I Write.. 24
I Knew Not 25
Keeping Score... 26
Childish 27
Meanderings.. 28
About the Author 42

Here I Stand

I felt the calmness of water trickling through my hands.
The warmth of my feet, pushing into sand.
The tranquility of sunlight warming my skin.
The coolness of rain, washing away my sin.
The air cradled me in a warm breeze.
My ears caressed by the sound of swaying trees.
My eyes dazzled by beams of electric light.
To stars shimmering in the stillness of night.
Here I stand, in cool brown earth.
Here I stand, a lamb by birth.
Here I stand, below the sky's diaphanous haze.
Here I stand, before the moon's luminous gaze.
Tethered to the soil by reality's tenuous grip...
Eyes wide open with a trembling lip.

Birds of Prey

Birds of prey
with a digital face
circling above
don't make a mistake.
They'll swoop right in
to peck off your face
what power it gives them
to see you disgraced.
The birds of prey
will swoop right in
to point out your flaws
and call out your sins
they'll even warp the meaning
of your words
an entire flock
they're hostile little birds....
They'll peck out your eyes
and even much worse
and when they're done,
they'll devour your corpse.

Birds of prey
look for the meek
to strengthen themselves
with the taste of your meat.

Birds of prey
with a digital face
Oh, what power it gives them
to see you disgraced.

2

Digital Smiles

It is far too easy
for a lie to become the truth...
for perception to become reality
in a world connected by digital strands
threads that weave us together
to cut us apart
into lines of data
cookies, ads,
and digitized hearts.

Subscriptions and apps
play their part
our digital smiles gleaming
as we share our arts.

We lie and we lie
our digital smiles beaming
Perception is reality.
Perhaps, we are dreaming?

Digital smiles
cold and aloof
I'm not as beautiful in person,
I'm missing a tooth!
Digital smiles
ring absent of truth,
Where is my data?
It's gone in a *poof!*

The Day is Nigh

I dreamed of yesterday
on a whim
I'd grown so old
stretched on a limb
the day is nigh
perhaps a bit dim
joy today
tomorrow, grim.

I lay in my bed
on a blanket of grass
that used to be green
in days long past.

My time has come
and the day is nigh
when it is time for us
to say our goodbyes
with a sadness that overwhelms
with a wave of grief
knowing our time in this life
is far too brief.

4

Out of the Heart the Soul Speaks

Out of the heart the soul speaks.
Out of the soul the spirit seeks.
Out of sadness the soul weeps.
Out of abundance, the soul reaps.
It empties itself like a river into the sea
Out of the heart, the soul speaks.
It replenishes itself like a mountain spring,
with all of the beauty and splendor that goodness brings.
Out of the heart, the soul speaks.
Out of the soul, the spirit seeks.
Out of love, the heart leaps.
In despair, the soul leaks.
Out of the heart the soul speaks.

"I'm Little and I'm Scared"
Hind's Story

I'm little and I'm scared,
a lamb unspared
when missiles shelled
my world unprepared
crumbling in despair,
by the cruel and unfair.

"I'm little and I'm scared. Please come and get me..."

Like a firefly in a jar
crushed in a car,
my family afar,
I don't know where we are...

The tanks are humming,
the drummers are drumming,
they kill or they hurt me,
and now they desert me,
shoot or they burn me,
war is among us,
why do they hurt us?
Eradicate us,
and no one in the world is coming.
I'm so little and scared,
I'm not being spared.
Please come and get me.

The paramedics are coming
And now they're succumbing,

6

The weapons are aiming
The ambulance is flaming,
and now, no one is coming.

I'm little and I'm scared,
There's smoke in the air,
The buildings are crumbling and unfolding.

In terror and despaired,
my life wasn't spared.

Where is my bear?
Does anyone care,
that I need my mommy to hold me?

Disinformation

Disinformation
is information of a most insidious kind.
It disguises itself as truth
to render us blind.
It preys on our fears
plants itself in our minds
rinse and repeat
two thousand and twenty times.

It provokes us to anger,
sowing distrust
spurring us to acts
of wanton bloodlust.

It's not what we seek, but often what we find.

Disinformation
is information of a most insidious kind.

Meta News

Meta news
is giving me the blues
celebrity clues
social media hues
he said/she said/they said
we said
"ha ha ha"
We dread.
Is...*we dead?*

Surreal...
When reaction to the news.
Became news.
How meta.

We examine ourselves from afar,
without introspection
or self-reflection.

An Inconvenient Sacrifice

Someone told us
about a disease
that spread itself
through a gentle breeze
or sometimes a cough
or even a sneeze...
and enters the lungs
through the air we breathe
left us yearning for loved ones
and much bereaved.
For some it left them
much aggrieved,
so we hung our heads,
and pretended it left
as it choked, grabbed
and stole our breath.
The rich gets richer
the dead gets deader
we sacrificed little
to make it all better.
An inconvenient sacrifice
let us hope it fades
until it drags us
into our unmarked graves.

Whose Truth?

Seeing is believing
at my own expense.
I'm a little misguided.
Nay, I am dense.
Perception is reality.
Reality, intense.
Nay, I'll stay silent.
The truth gives offense.
Tell me *your truth*,
Nay, I'll relent.
Told my own truth.
Today, I'll repent.

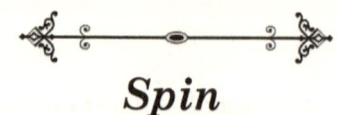

Spin

A spin of the words
to make you believe
How catchy they are!
Designed to deceive.
The spinning of the words
to make you perceive
such flashy little words.
Oh, the lies that they weave!

Here

Why is this world so painful?
Why do I cling to it so?
What am I so afraid of?
Why am I afraid to go?
I know it does not love me,
it even tells me so...
*and yet I am still **here**,*
ever unwilling to flow.
Flow into the abyss,
an abyss I cannot know.
An abyss that comforts in darkness
In a blanket as cold as snow.

"US"

There are two of me now
wherever I look
is it my shadow?
or is it a crook?
 figment, a pigment
an imagination game
a figment, a pigment,
caressing my name
it stood beyond my light
to bask in my shadow
to stand in my footprint
but its feet were too shallow
it sang out its words
but its message was hollow

I spun to my left
it aggressively followed
spun a web of lies
and foolishly wallowed.

There are two of me now
wherever I look
it wasn't my shadow.
perhaps it's a crook?

14

Night I Come Hither to Thee

Lay down my sickened heart
Night I come hither to thee
christened by a blanket of stars
scattered into the sea.
Night I come hither to thee.
Cool loose earth to blanket me
sweet time don't forget me
as I lay down to sleep
for I am done.
A waning wave roaming a morning sea
from thence I wither
and hither to thee
scorched dirt to nebulous sky
whisper sweet spirit
purge venom from my tongue
lay down my sickened heart
for thither I go, and hither I come
put down these gentle words
for there I seek
from this I thither
and hither to thee
sweet night, I come hither to thee.

I Was Never Here

A splinter of grass
its sharpened blade
dulls with time
as memories fade
it comes and goes
as seasons change
strengthens with life
in fresh spring rain
it does not whine
or tremble with fear
it does not know
it was never here.

In the black of night
it glitters afar
a fire burning
in a dying star
its golden embers
ignites the ether
a catastrophic explosion
it doesn't remember
its fiery rage
twinkle gently
as memories fade
it does not whine
or tremble with fear
it does not know
it was never here.

When pain flashed
across my temple
my body shook
and my fingers trembled
I sat and stared
into the abyss
thinking of all
I will come to miss
as my entire being
ceased to exist.
A passing memory
that fades with time
that even my life
was never mine.
I did not know
love was not real
or in a hundred years
I would disappear.
my entire being
did not exist
that it slipped through
time
into a darkened abyss
I knew not that I,
would disappear
I knew not that I,
was never here.

16

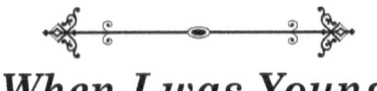

When I was Young

When I was an infant
I crawled because I could not walk
When I was an infant
I babbled because I could not talk

When I was young
I ignored my good health
When I was old
I'd do anything,
even spend my good wealth.

When I was old
I babbled because I could not talk.
When I was old
I crawled because I could not walk.

When I was young
I wanted to stay young.
When I was old
I yearned to grow older.

Saturate

I smell raindrops
saturate my air
fall from my sky
pour down on my hair
wet me now
lay me down
when you're near

Don't leave me standing
in the blistering sun
touched by its light
but loved by no one

Love my heavenly body
saturate my skin
drown my naked soul
and wet me with sin

Forget me not
pour down your love
make my grey skies blue
please leave me the sun
please leave me with you

I quake with remembrances
the tenderness of your
touch
and ache with the
emptiness
of loving too much

Have mercy

your touch was electric

sweet against my flesh
rain onto a desert flower
petals caressed

But memories leave me
in too cold a place
to shiver in dusk's dull light
absent of grace

You leave me standing here
in eve's declining sun
touched by its dwindling
light but loved by no one.

18

Curtain Call

Alas, the grand finale.
My exit from the stage.
as I slip through the bars
of my spaghetti-stringed cage,
I race from the darkness
time forgot me not
it unraveled me still
and played back my life
in a black and white reel.
I thought I died
in 2019.
my soul still trapped
in a kaleidoscope of dreams.

Curtain call
my exit from the stage
forget me not
but turn the last page.
Forget me not
hold your boos and awes
as I exit stage left
to sparse applause.

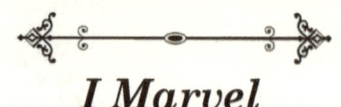

I Marvel

I marvel.
At the subtle call of the wind.
A mountain stands in defiance
where a river bends.
I marvel.
The sun rises
The smell of dew
A hummingbird's wings
The sun bidding us adieu.

I marvel.
As time slips through my grasp
I marvel.
At days long past.

I marvel.
A creek's steady stream.
I marvel.
In a haze of sunlight's
unyielding beams.

I marvel
A meadow's colorful bloom.
I marvel.
At the beauty of life,
from within my tomb.

Whisper

I am alone
On an empty stage
I am alone
In my own rage
I am alone
On an empty page,
I am alone
In my old age

Dead Roses

I can see my face in the gutter's mirror
reflecting my skin
now dry and withered.
My withered body lay dead in the street
my once praised beauty lies suffering in defeat.
Uprooted and discarded
I lay broken hearted
with my once fragrant skin
and limbs in the wind...

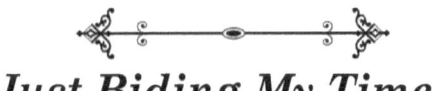

Just Biding My Time...

Death is freedom from the daily grind
we are wary to leave our children behind
when our bodies die,
what happens to our minds?
Death is freedom from the daily grind.
What happens when we are put to earth
and our bodies return to dust and dirt?
Will God tally up our worth?
Or will we return in another birth?
I look to stars, when they align
hoping for just a little sign...
That death is freedom from the daily grind.
We miss most of our days
working like slaves
building concrete giants
or office-like caves
getting the blues
just watching the news
paying our taxes
and paying our dues
in the end I wonder
what's on the other side
maybe I'll sleep
as I bide my time...
Death is freedom from the daily grind.

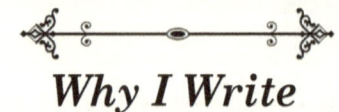

Why I Write

I flicker out of existence
my blue heart bleeds
a flame without oxygen
I do not breathe...
Dare I forsake,
The beauty
God made me to create
That comes to me
in a blinding light
and warms my soul
and my heart at night
or leaves me colder
than blocks of ice
chiseled from glaciers
cooled by a northern sky.
Til it comes to me
in a warm summer breeze
like streams of sunshine
beaming through trees
my heart becomes puddles
of shimmering streams
my poor soul flowing,
to barren land
lest my pen is writing
and moved by my hand.

I Knew Not

I saw not
what I was supposed to see.
Ignorance is bliss.
I miss the old me.

I knew not
what I was supposed to know.
I closed my third eye.
It was only for show.

I felt not
what I was supposed to feel
I sat in the dark
to shield my good heel.

I closed my third eye
to protect my good heel
Ignorance is bliss
So I'll eat a full meal.

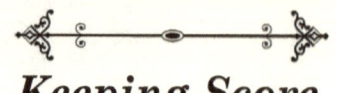

Keeping Score

Simulation theory
made me weary
we forgot what
Is real.
As we live in our dream
World
fighting cyber wars
for politicians
to gain political scores
lost and won arguments
of utter meaninglessness
We forgot to live
in the real World.

Childish

You laugh and joke
at someone's expense
you've forgotten your manners
and give much offense.
Jeering at others,
"Oh, look at this pic!"
Spouting cruel words
to make yourselves feel good
for an "lol" or click
new followers lining up
to join your 'clique"
Did it make you feel big?
In the real world,
you are so small.
With your digital smile,
you can finally stand tall.
Or pretend to be special
behind your digital wall.
Oh the foolery,
the smallish ways.
clamoring for clicks,
digital hearts, likes
while using fake pics.
Oh how childish we are,
anything to be seen
how utterly childish
it is to be "mean"
beyond the cowardly shadow
of a digital screen.

Meanderings...

Following the Leader

The world could do without followers.
The world could do without leaders.

Leaders are charismatic people.
With their charisma, leaders guide their followers
and ultimately the world down a darkened path.
There is only one way to stop them.
Without followers, there is no one to carry out
their dark misdeeds or anyone
to empower their cruelty.

The world could do without leaders.
The world could do without followers.

29

Time becomes a precious resource when you begin to understand how quickly it slips through your fingers.

Time is the one resource that never replenishes itself. Each second that passes by slips into the abyss.

Another follows, then it too, is gone forever.

Tick. Tick. Tick. It is the sound of a hand subtracting yet another second from my life with each second that ticks by.

Don't bare your soul to the world and expect to be loved. I learned a long time ago that people will hurt you if given the authority. I doubt they know why, but I imagine the power of hurting someone vulnerable, a stranger, or perhaps a famous person is intoxicating to some.

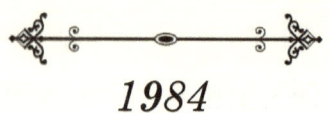

1984

I've learned to embrace invisibility.
To cherish it.

Behind every digital smile
a sinister face is smirking.

We lack filters and boundaries.
Our opinions carelessly vomited into spaces
where they are unwanted.
We have lost our sense of civility and
propriety.

Chivalry is also dead.
So is society.

In our lust for "truth"
we embrace lies...
ever willing to believe anything
that masquerades as a secret
yearning to be exposed.

37

We've become a people
unwilling to save or help others
at the slightest inconvenience to ourselves.

There is a strange fixation with murder in movies, books, and storytelling.
The more brutal the more fascinated and mesmerized viewers become.
Why is fictional (and nonfictional) murder a form of entertainment?

Social media is an endless cycle of strangers screaming opinions at each other while losing their grip on reality.

1974

There is hope and beauty in the world.
It is my wish that we can explore deeper and
more meaningful ways to engage each other
with the light of love in our hearts.

About the Author

E. Hughes is a novelist and writer of more than twenty-five years and has over twenty published works in multiple genres from fiction, nonfiction, poetry, and children's books to date. Her latest offering is *Digital Smiles*, her final work of poetry, released in February 2024. Hughes is scheduled to release *Reality Unbound*, a nonfiction, and *Kissing Henry*, a YA graphic novel. Hughes is also the author of *Sixth Iteration, Time and the Multi-Universe: A philosophy of time and time travel, Starting Your First Patio Garden: A Coffee Table Book, the Penelope Children's books series, Disappear, Love, A Mediterranean Romance, Business as Usual, Infatuation, The Sapphire Chronicles, Hello (a screenplay), Beyond the Plain,* and other works. Hughes is also an avid observer of cultural and societal idiosyncrasies.

E. Hughes was born in 1974, attended college in Chicago, IL where she majored in Art and Liberal Arts in the 1990s and early 2000s. She has previously lived on the west coast and in Las Vegas, NV but spends most of her time in the Midwest where she writes and publishes fiction novels, nonfiction, and children's books. Her love of writing began at the age of 8 years-old after winning a poetry contest. She knew then that she had the writing bug and would grow up to become a writer. Hughes was even more inspired after a seating next to Dr. Maya Angelou and meeting Gwendolyn Brooks, among many other notable authors in 1999 at a writer's conference in Chicago. Listening to Dr. Angelou, who was the keynote speaker of the evening was the highlight of her college years. Hughes would later accomplish her goal in 2003 with the release of her first poetry book, *Beyond the Plain*. She would eventually release her second book, a collection of short stories the same year, followed by twenty more novels and books in the years to come.

In addition to a decades-long career in writing, the focus of her career has been in education, publishing, and marketing. From 2012-2018, Hughes taught publishing and marketing in Madison, Wisconsin at Madison College and as an instructor at University of Wisconsin's Writers' Institute in 2017.

Hughes is acknowledged by, and continues her work with hundreds of writers across the United States and abroad from Canada, to the United Kingdom, to other parts of Europe, and Africa. Special education has also been a cause near to her heart. She has previously worked in K-12 special education at the local school district and in management at United Cerebral Palsy (UCP) of Greater Dane for 0-3 special education serving Dane County.

E. Hughes is also an avid gardener, painter, and hobbyist jewelry designer. She is a spouse and mother to four adult children.